CELEBRATING THE FAMILY NAME OF SUN

Celebrating the Family Name of Sun

Walter the Educator

Silent King Books
a WhichHead Entertainment Imprint

Copyright © 2024 by Walter the Educator

All rights reserved. No part of this book may be reproduced in any manner whatsoever without written permission except in the case of brief quotations embodied in critical articles and reviews.

First Printing, 2024

Disclaimer

This book is a literary work; the story is not about specific persons, locations, situations, and/or circumstances unless mentioned in a historical context. Any resemblance to real persons, locations, situations, and/or circumstances is coincidental. This book is for entertainment and informational purposes only. The author and publisher offer this information without warranties expressed or implied. No matter the grounds, neither the author nor the publisher will be accountable for any losses, injuries, or other damages caused by the reader's use of this book. The use of this book acknowledges an understanding and acceptance of this disclaimer.

Celebrating the Family Name of Sun is a memory book that belongs to the Celebrating Family Name Book Series by Walter the Educator. Collect them all and more books at WaltertheEducator.com

USE THE EXTRA SPACE TO DOCUMENT YOUR FAMILY MEMORIES THROUGHOUT THE YEARS

SUN

Sun, a name of radiant glow,

A beacon bright, a light to show.

Through ancient lands and skies so high,

Its brilliance spans the earth and sky.

A name that holds the dawn's first hue,

The warmth of morning, fresh and new.

It rises strong with hope each day,

Guiding hearts along their way.

From fertile fields to rivers wide,

The Sun name flows like a steady tide.

Its roots are deep, its reach is vast,

A family strong through ages past.

In scholars' minds and artists' hands,

The Sun name builds, it boldly stands.

With wisdom sharp and dreams that soar,

It paves a path forevermore.

The golden rays of Sun bestow

A legacy that will always grow.

Through trials faced and mountains climbed,

The Sun name stands, a mark of time.

In every heart, a spark is born,

A flame that lights each coming morn.

The Sun name shines, it leads the way,

A constant guide, come night or day.

Its spirit dances on the breeze,

In rustling leaves, in whispering seas.

The Sun name speaks of joy and grace,

A timeless bond, a cherished place.

From ancient scrolls to modern dreams,

The Sun name glows in endless streams.

It carries hope, it builds anew,

A legacy noble, bold, and true.

Like sunlight breaking through the storm,

The Sun name thrives in every form.

With strength and love, it leads the fight,

Transforming shadows into light.

So here's to Sun, a name so bright,

A symbol bold, a source of light.

Its story told, its journey long,

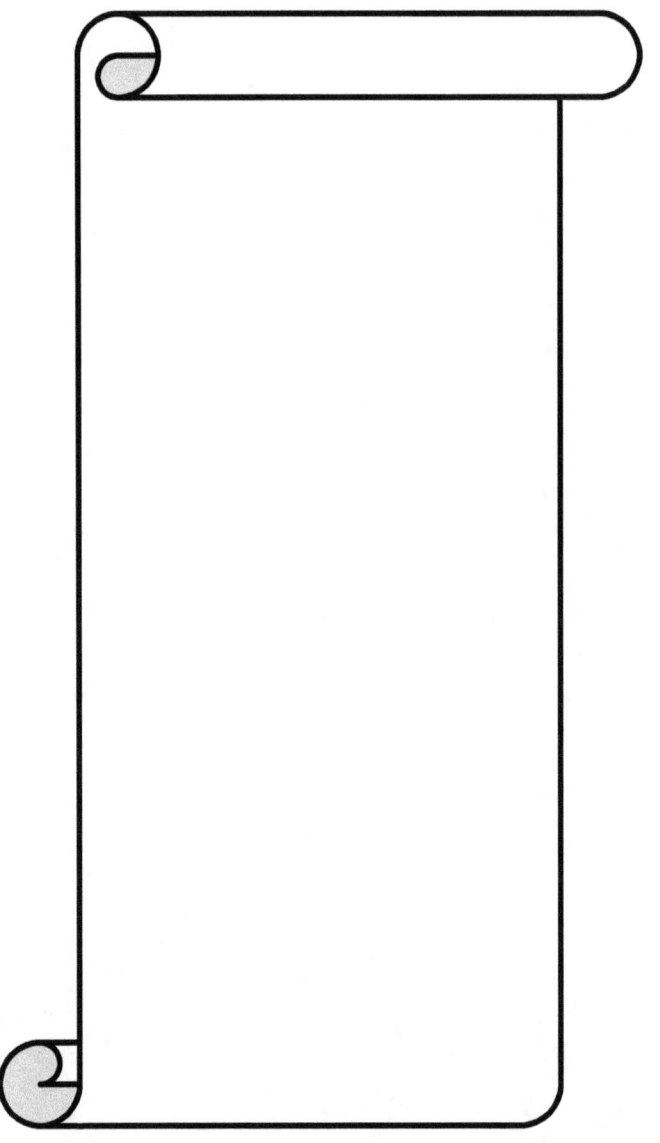

A family proud, a name so strong.

ABOUT THE CREATOR

Walter the Educator is one of the pseudonyms for Walter Anderson. Formally educated in Chemistry, Business, and Education, he is an educator, an author, a diverse entrepreneur, and he is the son of a disabled war veteran. "Walter the Educator" shares his time between educating and creating. He holds interests and owns several creative projects that entertain, enlighten, enhance, and educate, hoping to inspire and motivate you. Follow, find new works, and stay up to date with Walter the Educator™ at WaltertheEducator.com

www.ingramcontent.com/pod-product-compliance
Lightning Source LLC
LaVergne TN
LVHW012052070526
838201LV00082B/3924